Advance Praise

From the first page—that is, the table of contents—I wanted to read *Felled*: "Fall" precedes the compelling "Being Specific in my Dating Profile"—and within are lyrical notes that more than satisfied my curiosity. With visceral imagery and raw emotional depth, Vitcova grapples with trauma, memory, and how the past shows up in the body's present. Unafraid to go deeply toward emotional and physical vulnerability, these poems come to life with a voice that is both tender and unflinching. We see precise images like, "Hard is the edge of a shadow attached to a blade that drips," alongside moments of stark honesty—"I barely can say goodbye without crying." The poems here embody both pain and a quiet resilience in a way that that feels at once familiar and strikingly original. *Felled* is a collection to hold onto.
—**Jeanine Walker**, author
The Two of Them Might Outlast Me

Laura Vitcova's collection *Felled* is a distillation, a concision of the almost-devastatingly-so emotionally wrought bodyscape of longing and loss, desire and sorrow; here, a guitar is plucked "until a song drips from its sound hole," "flowers bloom at the ends of filaments," and all seems "a splintered love." These poems warm—and chill—only the way want can. "In a bed that smells like a bouquet," Vitcova's *Felled* picks up the knife that "cut breath flutters."
—**Flower Conroy**, author
Snake Breaking Medusa Disorder
Greenest Grass

Felled

poems by

Laura Vitcova

Finishing Line Press
Georgetown, Kentucky

for Geraldine and Hy

Copyright © 2025 by Laura Vitcova
ISBN 979-8-89990-128-7 First Edition
All rights reserved under International and Pan-American Copyright Conventions. No part of this book may be reproduced in any manner whatsoever without written permission from the publisher, except in the case of brief quotations embodied in critical articles and reviews.

Publisher: Leah Huete de Maines
Editor: Christen Kincaid
Cover Art: Laura Vitcova
Author Photo: Chris Courtney
Cover Design: Elizabeth Maines McCleavy

Order online: www.finishinglinepress.com
also available on amazon.com

Author inquiries and mail orders:
Finishing Line Press
PO Box 1626
Georgetown, Kentucky 40324
USA

Contents

Fall   1

Being Specific in my Dating Profile   3

Electricity at Atmospheric Pressure   5

Dear Lisa   7

For the Altar   9

Crumbs   11

In a Pandemic   13

This Year Nothing is Junk   15

Beloved   17

In Iceland   19

In a House with an Old Man   21

The Sea   23

By Design   25

Elegy for the Infusion   27

Mt. Tamalpais   29

Shema   31

Felled   33

Index of Images   34

Acknowledgments   35

Fall

A golden shovel after Eduardo C. Corral

I try to remember the who, when he
peels off clothes, lets the cold air hit, calls
the middle of my belly a drinking well, makes me
sit like a bird, lick him like a scarecrow
while the unsilence settles in
like the blinding green of Oregon
like the kind of chance he
sticks in his pocket. I was picked
ripe, it was September, the season for apples.

Being Specific in my Dating Profile

My body holds onto the memory
of being singled out for extermination,
of the forced labor to my mother's bed,
of using a blow dryer smoldering,
to look like a femme fatale
while burning my scalp in the process.

I'm attached to little things like a dust
that's difficult to clean. A splintered love.
I barely can say goodbye without crying.
I am looking for a falconer to tether my legs,
watch me magically transform an ache
into an electrode, make what's stalled beat again.

Electricity at Atmospheric Pressure

because the human body is conductive
flowers bloom at the ends of filaments

the aluminum can pulled through party
ice weeps in my hand, condenses water

your eyes thin the back of my neck
like a knife growing too close

a shiver drips down the skin
of my collar, the button up

gathering sweat, my body
jolts fusing flesh like solder

I heard that to stop connecting is to die
sooner. I am a plasma globe

voltage in an evacuated glass tube
a cavity filled with noble gasses

engaging enough space to transmit
a single tendril when touched

Dear Lisa

Do you remember how we'd cut ourselves
into bits so we could fit inside those skinny jeans?
How we'd hyperventilate for kicks
blackout and crumple against the bedroom door?
Bloodletting like hometown flora
falling under the sun and psilocybin
I don't remember the honeysuckle
betraying its scent. I only remember a silhouette—
my mother's favorites were hydrangeas—
but you remember exactly the face of the boy
in the baby blue Beetle who raped me.
Remember how we'd pull petals and say *he loves me,
he loves me not* until the daisies were left
just as stems and stigmas?

For the Altar

Because you can saw me in half
Create the illusion of chatting with my head
Move my heart to the middle of my thigh
Sense which parts quiver when touched;

Because you tug like how a magician
Pulls rabbits out, snatches coins from
Makes sunflowers come blossoming
Out of silk scarves like wet chakras;

I will toss water over jasmine in vase,
cross a wire with a saddle and nut,
Pluck the guitar, turn pegs 'til it's tuned,
Strum until a song drips from its sound hole.

Crumbs

A drop off
a sweet bun
fallen between planks
the hungry mouse
survives on
fairly little
scurries room to room
for a wee bit broken
just enough to wet
an open mouth.

In a Pandemic

a poisonous
breath howls

wind and sand
across lips

longing to fall
onto something

warm and porous
moisture spits

shore shaped
waiting

barring hope
the earth cannot die.

This Year Nothing is Junk

Feel certitude washing…rolling over little fingers in the surf… But what if little fingers are drowning? *Hold each object and listen to what sparks joy, let go of what doesn't.* But what if the wanting suffocates joy so joy can't answer back? What if what sparks joy is a miniature glass white dog with raised black spots? What if the miniature pink poodle plays with the miniature glass Dalmatian and they're stuck in a pose? What if I still weep for the pink, the mud, the afterschool specials? What if sparking joy is too dangerous because the smell of gasoline still gets me high? What if my chest contains razor blades and what comforts on nights when the stars are too bright is a joy that feels like a dagger? What if he never really wanted me but a small coat of dirt feels warm? What if the rock picked by the sandy haired boy as a token of his affection still sits on my desk, caresses like an anticline, bends time like froth? What if it all just occupies the same space and the shaking in my thorax is where music meets what's bruised and it's ok? What if I simply need a hand to hold on to before I let go?

Beloved

When your beloved uses all their strength,
Nails stuttering across wooden planks,
Frantically clicking at the floor to fall at your feet,
Panic is an option, so is unsurrendered love.
I'm sorry, please forgive me, thank you, I love you.

Hard is the edge of a shadow attached to a blade that drips.
Precious are the suns that move seconds across your face.
Water clinging to your muzzle in my hands, panting,
Collars and leashes and never-ending love
In a bed that smells like a bouquet,

Because you let me wash your fur
And kill you with compassion at the moment of no choice,
When wildness returns with metal trays and scissors.
Only you, only you,
In the air I hear you breathing.

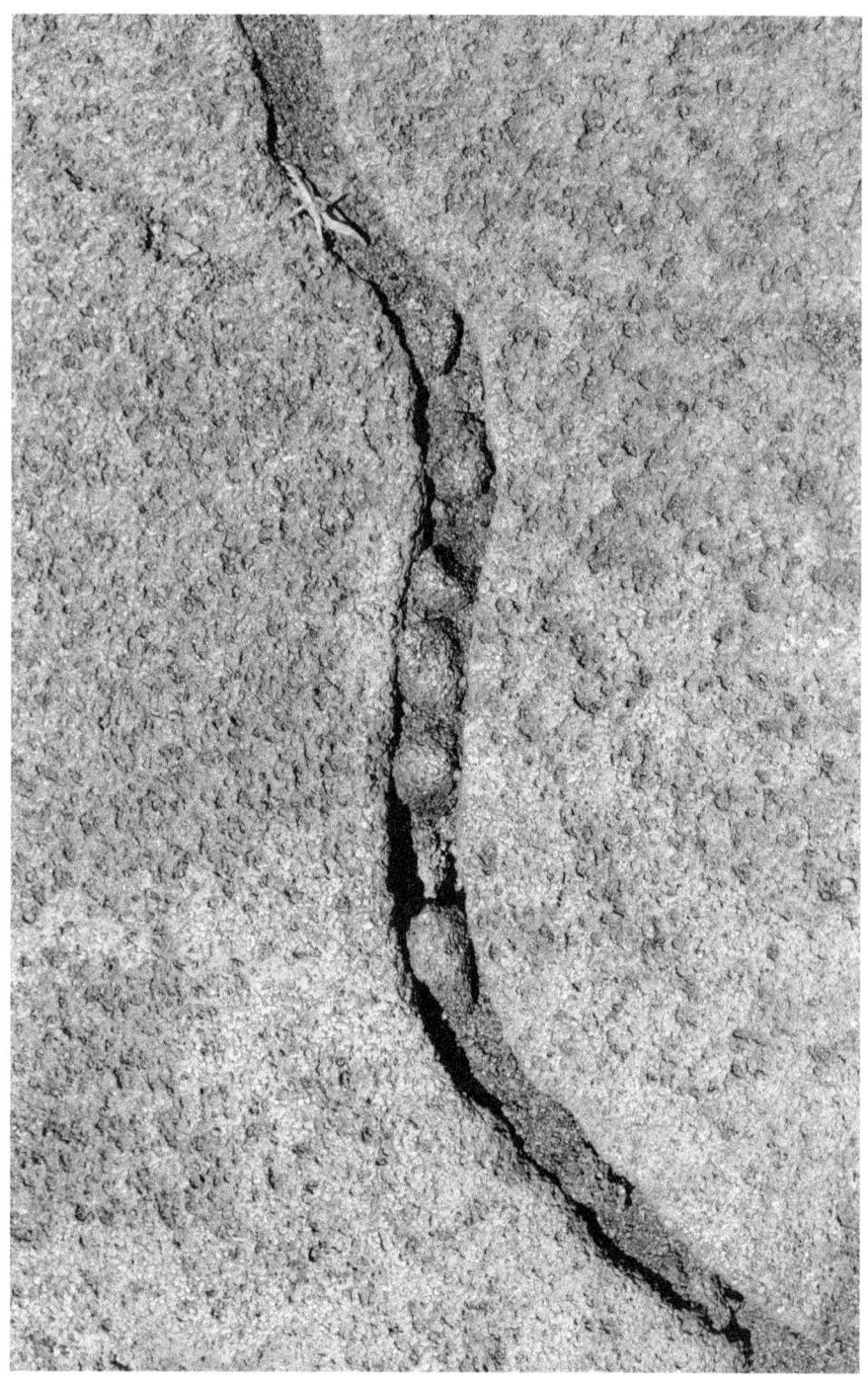

In Iceland

lava swells and spews
like a cut artery rages
gives birth
rhythmically spits rock
skinned into cliffs
icy wind splits the sky
relentless tides
I lay my neck
across the wooly moss
we are so easily crushed.

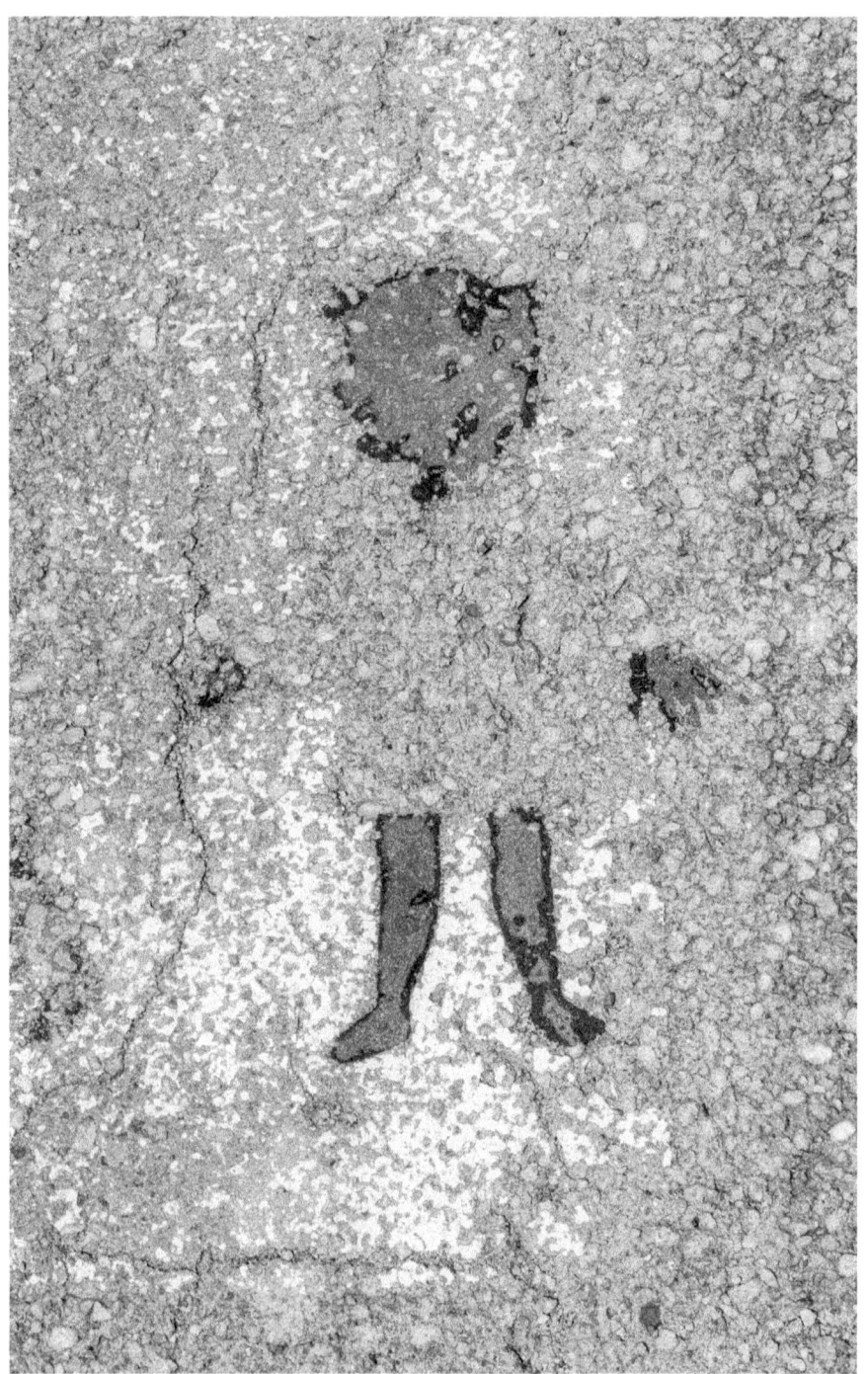

In a House with an Old Man

I caught his head
pressed against the door
hard like a crowbar
listening to me having sex.
I opened the bedroom
and there he was, all red
I felt—
sorry
I didn't know how deep
my moisture burned
like steam whistling
the lid off
his loneliness.
I just needed a place
to stay seventeen,
because you married a guy
who didn't want a child
at home listening.

The Sea

Scratching perfectly centered letters, diamond tips
lick metal discs. I am waiting for a dog tag to finish
engraving when a five-year old drops a goldfish.
The pet sloshes inside its watertight balloon,
Mamma smacks the side of the little girl's head
and she bursts.
Lightning takes just seconds to tell thunder when to hit
so I begin to count until she begins to shake.
When a smash happens to a small soft surface
the laws of physics twist fleshy like twine
time becomes an affect of, a repercussion of
generations winding back to the original strike.
Mamma pays, carries her out to wail
mumbling, "She tried to murder the fish."

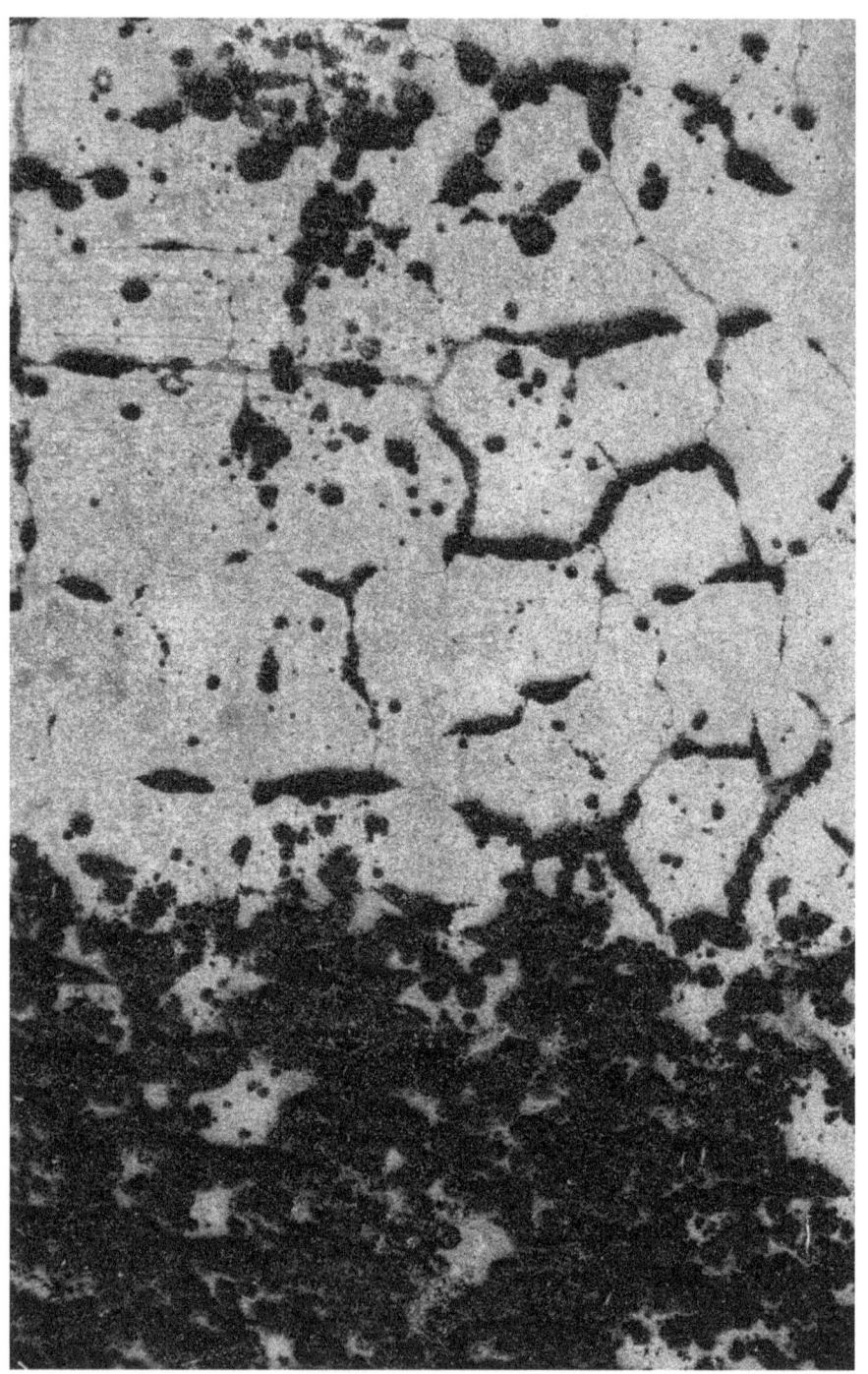

By Design

White space. Balls
with more weight
on one side. Reason
for the slope
slanted mobs of flesh.
A washer hissing
inside the machine
pondering if (a + b) equals
freedom from the illusion of
cracked binary code:
a pineal gland, a body
in Tupperware, pulp,
a Popsicle jibbing.

Elegy for the Infusion
    "...live the day like there's no tomorrow." —Stefanie Keys

IV stands with tubes pouring into folks
sitting with their person, you putting on the numbing

cream, cranking up Steely Dan's Dirty Work,
handing me a copy of Bernie on the cover of Time.

I said *when you get better we'll do this or that*
but the clothes in your house were still in a wet pile,

one white shirt was hanging, light
from the window was making the cotton translucent.

I was preparing a tuna fish sandwich,
picking up cutting boards and knives,

opening cabinets
while you sat at the wooden table

next to a vase of pink and blue hydrangeas
from your garden. I wanted to capture everything—

video you singing, stay, stop time,
not care about the traffic.

Mt. Tamalpais

Walking on a path
after yoga class
heart chakra opening
upward facing dog
the gilded edges
of harlequins, buttercups
checker mallows
ballooning their tops
spitting 'cross grassland
freshly pressed bloom juice
barreling into my chest
golden wafers of pollen
floating vinyasana
swooning the air—
I am suspended
in standing tree pose
trying to describe
child's pose
but there are only
so many ways
to say yellow sun
owl as bell.

Shema

Shema yisrael, adonai eloheinu, adonai echad

On the edge of your bed bones exquisite ready resting
your arms on the arms of a hospice nurse your nails
still painted hair a shade of red your essence
hangs deflated on to the scent of earth.

a stethoscope on top of your vanity cancer dreams dusty long
eyeshadows lipsticks olive skin leather pumps polyester
perfume blouses stained tracing the sun the moon
your silvery eyes blue the color of a newborn's

a fistful of lemons the scent of citrus your lungs disintegrating
the scent of citrus the sun disintegrating
your tongue disintegrating
inside being eaten

sun falls pink on the fuzzy you sleep in resting
my head on your chest afraid to crush you
ancestors come cut breath flutters
yiddish landing in pieces

I thank your feet your wilted
womb singing
the shema.

Felled

My arms once covered in needles
like a porcupine, now boughs

sweeping the dirt beneath your feet
I pine for you, I am willing

to be eaten by mold, I am letting
worms bring water to lobes

breathing crimson rivers
no longer exhaling sulfur

I am as indifferent to termites
as I am to woodpeckers

but to you dear, there is no cap.
I have surrendered all thresholds.

My roots no longer hold onto dry soil
gale and gravity have instructed

me to fall now, and I am
kissing the earth over and over again.

Index of Images

All images are original photographs by Laura Vitcova. They are listed in the order they appear.

Hi'ilawe Falls, Waimea, Hawaii, 2021, cover
McGee Creek, Mono County, California, 2021
Ground Cover, Loudon, New Hampshire, 2019
Areca Palm Tree Roots, Hilo, Hawaii, 2021
Brush, Berkeley, California, 2019
Apples, Loudon, New Hampshire, 2019
Dried Mt. Charleston, Nevada, 2017
White Flower, Canterbury, New Hampshire, 2019
Lava Field, Volcanos National Park, Hawaii, 2021
Southern Andes, Machu Piccu, Peru, 2022,
Puu Loa, Volcanos National Park, Hawaii, 2021
Girl in Asphalt, Kanazawa, Japan, 2019
Lake Water, Mono County, California, 2021
Moss on Wall, Tokyo, Japan, 2019
Palm Frond, Hilo, Hawaii, 2021
Hydrangea, Canterbury, New Hampshire, 2019
Seaweed, Brjanslaekur, Iceland, 2021
Fallen Tree, County Donegal, Ireland, 2015
Body of a Tree, Portland, Oregon, 2020, back cover

ACKNOWLEDGMENTS

Many thanks to the editors of these journals in which these poems (often in earlier versions) first appeared:

Blue Earth Review "Electricity at nearly atmospheric pressure"
Epiphany "Beloved"
Grubstreet Journal "This Year Nothing is Junk"
Rue Scribe "In a pandemic"
Rogue Agent "Being more specific in my online dating profile"
The Orchards Poetry Journal "Felled"
The Shore Poetry "Shema"

Heartfelt thanks to friends and family who help fortify and guide me. Your time and attention as I worked on these poems is deeply appreciated. Special thanks to Katherine Stevenson for her editorial and moral support; to Mary Patterson for encouraging me to follow dreams; to Inga and Noel for always having my back; and to Jef Besinger for being an example of dedication to one's art. Thank you to my writing community for providing a place to share, for inspiring me with your poetry, and helping me grow. Special thanks to Melissa Strilecki for her empathy and humor; to Kryston Lopez for her enormous heart; and to Nicholas Jackson for numerous forms of support which includes surprising me with books. I owe a debt of gratitude to my teachers, especially Kim Addonizio, Taneum Bambrick, Maya C. Popa, Thea Matthews, Gabrielle Bates, Jeanine Walker, Flower Conroy and all the other poets who continue to fill me with inspiration.

Laura Vitcova was born in the San Francisco Bay Area and currently lives in the east bay city of Richmond. She is pursuing an MFA degree in Creative Writing at Pacific University and was awarded The MFA Merit Scholarship and The Washburn Scholarship. Her work has appeared in several online and print journals, including *The Shore Poetry, Blue Earth Review, Epiphany*. In her free time she travels with a camera, and sings. She credits her scruffy dog for her burgeoning interest in bird watching.

www.ingramcontent.com/pod-product-compliance
Lightning Source LLC
Chambersburg PA
CBHW020220090426
42734CB00008B/1147